KICK, JUMP, CHEER!

CHEERLEADING BASICS

BY SARA GREEN

BELLWETHER MEDIA • MINNEAPOLIS, MN

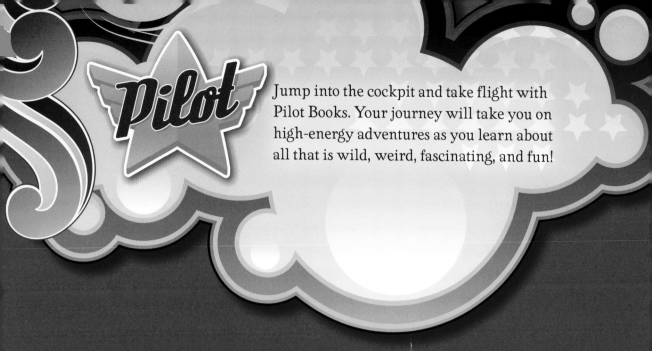

Jump into the cockpit and take flight with Pilot Books. Your journey will take you on high-energy adventures as you learn about all that is wild, weird, fascinating, and fun!

This edition first published in 2012 by Bellwether Media, Inc.

No part of this publication may be reproduced in whole or in part without written permission of the publisher.
For information regarding permission, write to Bellwether Media, Inc.,
Attention: Permissions Department,
5357 Penn Avenue South, Minneapolis, MN 55419.

Library of Congress Cataloging-in-Publication Data
Green, Sara, 1964—
Cheerleading basics / by Sara Green.
     p. cm. — (Pilot books : kick, jump, cheer!)
 Includes bibliographical references and index.
 Summary: "Engaging images accompany information about cheerleading basics. The combination of high-interest subject matter and narrative text is intended for students in grades 3 through 7"—
Provided by publisher.
 ISBN 978-1-60014-646-6 (hardcover : alk. paper)
 1. Cheerleading--Juvenile literature. I. Title.
 LB3635.G7415 2012
 791.6'4—dc22   2011010378

Printed in the United States of America, North Mankato, MN.

080111   1187

CONTENTS

RALLYING THE CROWD

It's time for the first football game of the season. Excited fans fill the bleachers. The cheerleaders are pumped up after weeks of practice. They are ready to **rally** the crowd with their **cheers** and jumps. The football team runs onto the field. Fans stand up and shout. The cheerleaders wave their **pom poms**. School spirit is high!

Does this make you want to jump to your feet and cheer? If you have a positive attitude, are a team player, and like performing in front of crowds, cheerleading might be the sport for you. As a member of a cheerleading **squad**, you will work hard, make new friends, and have fun. You will show team spirit and fire up fans every time you cheer!

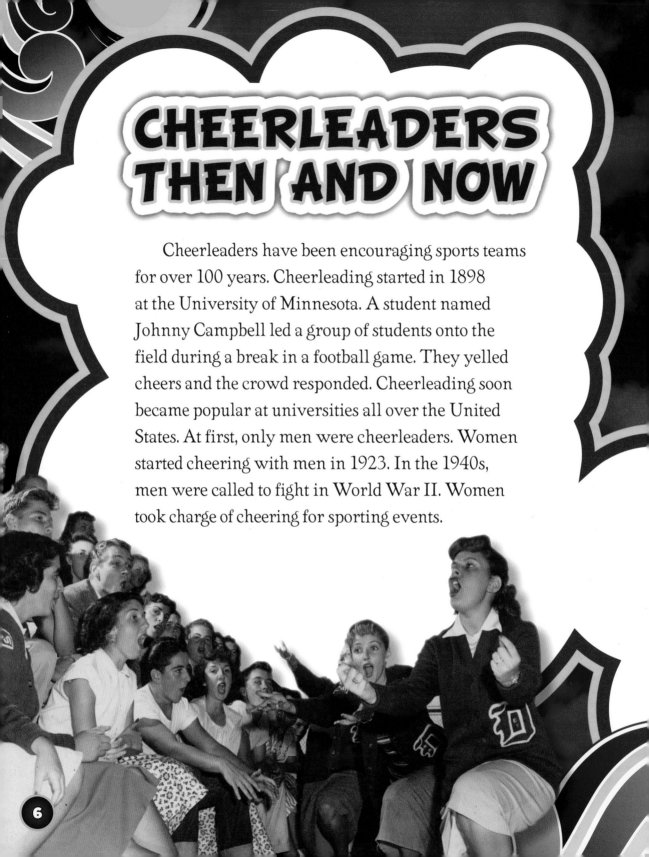

CHEERLEADERS THEN AND NOW

Cheerleaders have been encouraging sports teams for over 100 years. Cheerleading started in 1898 at the University of Minnesota. A student named Johnny Campbell led a group of students onto the field during a break in a football game. They yelled cheers and the crowd responded. Cheerleading soon became popular at universities all over the United States. At first, only men were cheerleaders. Women started cheering with men in 1923. In the 1940s, men were called to fight in World War II. Women took charge of cheering for sporting events.

JOHNNY CAMPBELL'S FIRST CHEER IN 1898 WENT LIKE THIS:
Rah, Rah, Rah!
Ski-U-Mah!
Hoo-Rah! Varsity!
Minn-e-so-tah!

Cheerleading has come a long way in 100 years. Cheerleaders do much more than just perform **chants** and cheers at sporting events. Their **routines** now include **tumbling** and dancing. Cheerleaders stay busy off the field too. They plan **pep rallies** and other activities that keep school spirit high.

A HEALTHY BODY AND ATTITUDE

Cheerleading is hard work. Cheerleaders need **flexibility**, strength, and **stamina**. You can increase your flexibility by stretching before and after any activity. This also prevents injuries. A coach can teach you how to stretch different muscles. Push-ups, pull-ups, and other simple exercises can help improve your strength. Jogging, dancing, and biking will boost your stamina. These activities are also fun to do with friends!

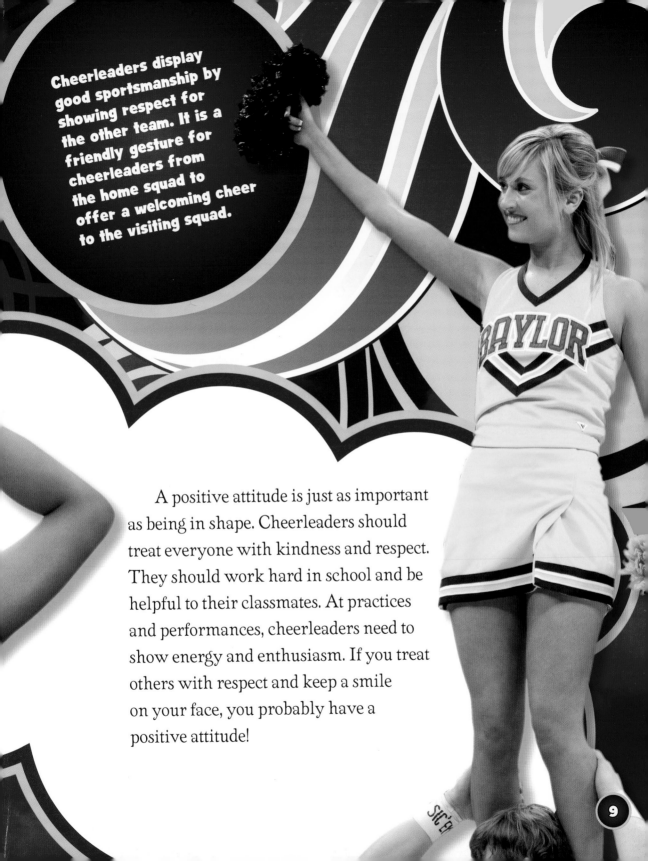

Cheerleaders display good sportsmanship by showing respect for the other team. It is a friendly gesture for cheerleaders from the home squad to offer a welcoming cheer to the visiting squad.

A positive attitude is just as important as being in shape. Cheerleaders should treat everyone with kindness and respect. They should work hard in school and be helpful to their classmates. At practices and performances, cheerleaders need to show energy and enthusiasm. If you treat others with respect and keep a smile on your face, you probably have a positive attitude!

Remember to smile!

TRYOUTS

All cheerleaders must go through **tryouts**. Preparing for tryouts takes time and practice. You should watch the squad to learn their moves and routines. Talk to the cheerleading coaches about what to expect at your tryout. Most squads schedule a practice week before they hold tryouts. Coaches often teach cheers, chants, and jumps during this week.

To prepare for your tryout, spend time practicing moves in front of a mirror. Keep your arm and leg movements sharp. Use a strong, clear voice when you yell chants and cheers. Remember to smile and make eye contact with the coaches during your tryout. Your confidence and enthusiasm will impress them!

CHANTS AND CHEERS

Chants and cheers fire up crowds and teams. Chants are short, catchy phrases that cheerleaders repeat several times. Fans love to yell chants along with cheerleaders. Chants often include sports terms such as "defense" and "offense." Cheerleaders usually yell chants during play. They clap their hands and stomp their feet to add rhythm to a chant.

Cheers are longer than chants. Cheerleaders usually perform them during breaks in play. Cheers often include the school's name, **mascot**, and team colors. Team pride soars when cheerleaders perform cheers!

A FOOTBALL GAME CHANT YOU CAN TRY!
Time to score!
Score! Score!
Six points more!

A FUN CHEER YOU CAN TRY!
We are [school colors]
Reaching for the stars!
[opposing team name]
Stand back!
[your team name] will attack!

JUMP RIGHT IN!

Cheerleaders also do jumps and **stunts** while they perform. Jumps add excitement to cheers. Cheerleaders do jumps when teams are being introduced and after great plays during a game. A basic jump is the **spread eagle**. Cheerleaders raise their arms in a "V" shape and spread their legs apart. Their bodies look like the letter "X." A harder jump is the **Herkie**. Cheerleaders kick one leg out straight to the side. They bend the other leg so that the knee is pointing toward the ground. An even more advanced jump is the **toe touch**. Cheerleaders kick their legs out wide and reach toward their toes. Sometimes the whole squad jumps together. Crowds love this eye-catching move!

toe touch

Pom poms became popular in the 1930s. They are also called pom pons. The name comes from the French word *pompon*, which means "tuft of ribbons."

THE THRILL OF THE STUNT

Cheerleading stunts thrill crowds with high-flying moves. Stunts involve climbing, lifting, and throwing. Each cheerleader has a special role in a stunt. **Bases** keep their feet on the ground. They lift, support, toss, and catch **flyers**. Bases are usually the strongest and tallest members of the squad. Flyers are usually the smallest. They must be able to balance on the bases. **Spotters** stand still and watch stunts. They help bases catch flyers. A popular beginner stunt is the **pony mount**. It uses a base, a flyer, and a spotter. A more advanced stunt is a **pyramid**. This uses several bases, spotters, and one or more flyers.

Stunts can be risky. To avoid injuries, coaches should be present when squads perform stunts. Squads should only do stunts that match their skill level.

flyer

spotter

base

SHOW YOUR SPIRIT

Cheerleaders try to look their best when they cheer. They smile whether their team is winning or losing. They wear matching uniforms in their team colors. Females wear skirts and fitted tops. Males wear shorts or pants and short-sleeve shirts. All cheerleaders wear shoes with a lot of support.

Cheerleaders use props and music to add color and excitement to their cheers. Songs with strong beats pump up the crowd. Cheerleaders shake pom poms and wave flags to catch the crowd's attention. They yell chants into **megaphones** to project their voices. Signs get the fans involved. Cheerleaders write words such as "GO" and "TEAM" on large signs. They flash each sign to a different section of the crowd. Each section yells its word. GO! TEAM!

megaphone

ARE YOU READY TO CHEER?

Cheerleading began as a way to encourage sports teams. Today, cheerleading is a demanding sport. Many cheerleaders are as fit as the athletes they support. It takes a huge commitment to be a great cheerleader. Squads often practice every day of the week.

Many cheerleaders attend tumbling and dance classes to develop their skills. All of the hard work pays off when cheerleaders feel the thrill of performing. Their energy, confidence, and spirit shine in every move they make. Both on and off the field, cheerleaders try to encourage others and show school spirit. Are you ready to join the squad?

GLOSSARY

bases—cheerleaders who lift and support flyers; bases keep their feet on the ground at all times during a stunt.

chants—short, repetitive phrases yelled during a game

cheers—long phrases yelled during routines; jumps and stunts often go along with cheers.

flexibility—the ability to stretch and move the body with ease

flyers—cheerleaders who stand on the bases and jump or are tossed into the air

Herkie—a jump where one leg is straight out to the side and the other leg is bent so the knee faces the ground

mascot—an animal or person used as a symbol of a group or team

megaphones—cone-shaped devices that project and direct voices over crowds

pep rallies—gatherings held before sporting events to boost school spirit and encourage sports teams

pom poms—colorful tufts made of plastic strips; cheerleaders shake pom poms during their routines.

pony mount—a stunt where a flyer sits on a base's back

pyramid—a stunt involving one or more flyers supported by bases

rally—to stir up and encourage enthusiasm

routines—sequences of moves that cheerleaders practice and perform

spotters—cheerleaders who are ready to help the bases catch the flyers

spread eagle—a jump where the arms and legs spread out to form the letter "X"

squad—a group of cheerleaders that works together as a team

stamina—the ability to do something for a long time

stunts—cheerleading moves that involve climbing and lifting; in some stunts cheerleaders are thrown into the air.

toe touch—a jump where the legs are spread wide; the right hand reaches toward the right foot, and the left hand reaches toward the left foot.

tryouts—events where people perform skills for coaches in order to make teams

tumbling—gymnastics skills such as cartwheels and handsprings; many cheerleading squads use tumbling in their routines.

TO LEARN MORE

At the Library

Gruber, Beth. *Cheerleading for Fun*. Minneapolis, Minn.: Compass Point Books, 2004.

Jones, Jen. *Cheer Basics: Rules to Cheer By*. Mankato, Minn.: Capstone Press, 2006.

Szwast, Ursula. *Cheerleading*. Chicago, Ill.: Heinemann Library, 2006.

On the Web

Learning more about cheerleading is as easy as 1, 2, 3.

1. Go to www.factsurfer.com.

2. Enter "cheerleading" into the search box.

3. Click the "Surf" button and you will see a list of related Web sites.

With factsurfer.com, finding more information is just a click away.

INDEX

The images in this book are reproduced through the courtesy of: Eliza Snow, front cover; James Hajjar, pp. 5, 7, 17, 20-21; Keystone/Getty Images, p. 6; Image Source/Getty Images, p. 8; Charlie Neibergall/AP Images, p. 9; Mike Orazzi/The Bristol Press, pp. 10-11; Getty Images, p. 13; Digital Vision/Getty Images, p. 15; Yellow Dog Productions/Getty Images, p. 18; Sports Illustrated/Getty Images, p. 19.